The

Corinthian

Mysteries

DAVID O'BRIEN

© 2022 by *David O'Brien*
ISBN: **978-1-7374242-7-7**

Scripture quotations are from these Bible versions:
- The New King James Version. Copyright © 1982 by Thomas Nelson, Inc. Used by permission. All rights reserved.
- The NEW AMERICAN STANDARD BIBLE®, Copyright © 1960,1962,1963,1968,1971,1972,1973,1975,1977, 1995, 2020 by The Lockman Foundation. Used by permission.
- The Holy Bible, English Standard Version copyright 2001, 2007, 2011, 2016 by Crossway Books and Bibles, a Publishing Ministry of Good News Publishers. Used by permission. All rights reserved.

Abbreviations:
NKJ – New King James Version
NASB – New American Standard Bible
ESV – English Standard Version

Blue Diamond Bookhouse

www.BlueDiamondBookhouse.com

Mystery: something not understood

Myth: a widely held but false belief or idea

"...and you will know the truth, and the truth will set you free."
–*The Lord Jesus*

"When the Spirit of truth comes, he will guide you into all the truth..."
–*The Lord Jesus*

Dedication

To the Lionesses whose arrival our King has long anticipated.

Contents

Introduction

The Scripture speaks of the power of human traditions. Jesus, the Word Himself, accused his countrymen of disempowering the Word of God *by their traditions* (Mark 7). The Word of God contains all of the power of God Himself in it, yet it could be drowned, stifled by human traditions. This ought to *scare us*.

We must question and doubt our traditions. There are good and profitable traditions, ones that help hold society and families together, but do they fully stand the test—this is the big question. Those that do not must be knocked down and cleared from the heart. Because God is looking for more, for the power found only in His Word. Its light rises like the sun of a glorious new day—one that has now come.

Indulge in this work. Dip your feet in first to consider the temperature of the water, that it's inviting—not shocking. Then brace yourself and jump in. It will be fun.

The Word of God is fun. Have unreserved fun with His Word. And let it dig up the treasures placed in human flesh, for you.

–David O'Brien

Chapter 1

The Corinthian Mysteries

The Bible's two Letters to the Corinthians are some of my favorites. Inside of them are scattered all kinds of treasures for us to hunt for and find. God has laden those books with Himself, his Light. And, as with all things of God, we must be cautious in our approach. We must be surgical and precise. There is always great treachery where great treasure is found.

We must also be persistent, and relentless till we find the Truth, like digging for precious stones in a mine. We must study. God is revealing Truth, all along the straight and narrow trail, to those who are proceeding forward and seeking it. So let us proceed forward.

The beginning of 1 Corinthians is very straight-forward. You can read it without hardly even having to consider its context. After that comes Chapter 7, verse 1:

Now concerning the things of which you wrote to me... (1 Corinthians 7:1, NKJV)

It's very important to understand that from this verse on:

1. Paul answers several questions the Corinthians had written to him previously about
2. Secondly, we do not have the letter(s) they had written to him

Knowing these two things, we can seek and find the hidden treasures in the rest of the book, and not miss them. When seeking treasures, we need the right tool for the job. Now we have it.

Now concerning the things of which you wrote to me: [It is] good for a man not to touch a woman. (1 Corinthians 7:1 NKJV)

Now concerning virgins: I have no commandment from the Lord; yet I give judgment as one whom the Lord in His mercy has made trustworthy. (1 Corinthians 7:25 NKJV)

Now concerning things offered to idols... (1 Corinthians 8:1 NKJV)

Therefore concerning the eating of things offered to idols... (1 Corinthians 8:4 NKJV)

He is answering their questions and addressing issues known to both of them.[1] Next, in 1 Corinthians 9 and 10, Paul teaches and shares his life for them as an example. Then comes Chapter 11. We can handle that chapter now. He starts in verse 2:

---

[1] He continues to address known issues to them through the rest of the book (e.g., 1Cor 11:17-18, 34; 1Cor 12:1; 1Cor 14:12; 1Cor 15:12; 1Cor 16:1; 1Cor 16:12).

2 Now I praise you, brethren, that you remember me in all things and keep the traditions just as I delivered [them] to you. (1 Corinthians 11:2 NKJV).

These are the traditions that passed the test, those he had received from the Lord and delivered to them. They were keeping them. BUT…next verse:

3 BUT I want you to know that the head of every man is Christ, the head of woman [is] man, and the head of Christ [is] God. (1 Corinthians 11:3 NKJV, emphasis mine)

He said, "But," and "I want you to know," because of an area of *disagreement* he had with them. Recognize that this sentence includes Paul's teaching about man, women and men, Christ, and God regarding headship—a subject most often abused and misunderstood. But we can heal that here.

NOW we can begin to understand the next several verses ☺. Clarity of vision will come to you through the cleansing that results. First, read and consider the whole passage, with the help of the fire/light in your spirit, and then we'll look at it together.

4 Every man praying or prophesying, having [his] head covered, dishonors his head. 5 But every woman who prays or prophesies with [her] head uncovered dishonors her head, for that is one and the same as if her head were shaved. 6 For if a woman is not covered, let her also be shorn. But if it is shameful for a woman to be shorn or shaved, let her be covered. 7 For a man indeed ought not to cover [his] head, since he is the image and glory of

3

God; but woman is the glory of man. 8 For man is not from woman, but woman from man. 9 Nor was man created for the woman, but woman for the man. 10 For this reason the woman ought to have [a symbol of] authority on [her] head, because of the angels.

11 Nevertheless [or "But rather,"], neither [is] man independent of woman, nor woman independent of man, in the Lord. 12 For as woman [came] from man, even so man also [comes] through woman; but all things are from God. 13 Judge among yourselves. Is it proper for a woman to pray to God with her head uncovered? 14 Does not even nature itself teach you that if a man has long hair, it is a dishonor to him? 15 But if a woman has long hair, it is a glory to her; for [her] hair is given to her for a covering. 16 But if anyone seems to be contentious, we have no such custom, nor [do] the churches of God. (1 Corinthians 11:4-16 NKJV)

I will point out many things here, so that this passage beams with light and value as the treasure it is. First of all, verse 4-10 clearly makes up a section. We need to understand *that* section in its context. Let's isolate it. Remember, do not feel intimidated by these verses, do not recoil in shame or anything, women. There is a healing taking place, and I want you to *KNOW* that God heals your heart and binds up your wound. Trust me, you won't be hurt here. Know that God would never suppress you—he's your Father who birthed the brilliance in you! Trust him enough now to let your heart settle and read this with an open mind.

Open the Book, and His Light will shine on your

inquisitive face—ooh the treasures you will discover in it!

Let's call verses 4-10, "The Section Under Examination," for the purpose of categorization:

4 Every man praying or prophesying, having [his] head covered, dishonors his head. 5 But every woman who prays or prophesies with [her] head uncovered dishonors her head, for that is one and the same as if her head were shaved. 6 For if a woman is not covered, let her also be shorn. But if it is shameful for a woman to be shorn or shaved, let her be covered. 7 For a man indeed ought not to cover [his] head, since he is the image and glory of God; but woman is the glory of man. 8 For man is not from woman, but woman from man. 9 Nor was man created for the woman, but woman for the man. 10 For this reason the woman ought to have [a symbol of] authority on [her] head, because of the angels. (1 Corinthians 11:4-11 NKJV)

We have established that Paul is not just writing in monologue style to the Corinthians. From Chapter 7 onward, he deals with them on things they both were aware of, based on their previous letter(s) to him. An outsider reading this must be keenly aware of this.

Above, I mentioned two tools to find the treasure here. Now here is another: in the original language of Greek, there is no punctuation, like we use in English. There are no quotation marks.

Now, let's consider this passage according to its crucial immediate context. Verses 2 and 3 immediately proceed verse 4:

2 Now I praise you, brethren, that you remember me in all things and keep the traditions just as I delivered [them] to you. 3 BUT I want you to know that the head of every man is Christ, the head of woman [is] man, and the head of Christ [is] God. (1 Corinthians 11:3 NKJV, emphasis mine)

Very important to note here is the "But" in verse 3. He just praised them, but there was an area of disagreement he had with them. Hence the word, "But." And he is teaching them something *they don't know.* He says, "I want you to know…." So they had an some ignorance that he was correcting. And then he reveals a mystery as to headship—I plan to dig into that diamond laden soil later in this book, which will also free you, Women of God, from traditional enemies. ☺ But for now, just notice that he is telling them what they don't know, that "the head of woman is man."

Now let's look at the verses immediately following The Section Under Examination, verses 11-12:

11 NEVERTHELESS [or "But rather"], neither [is] man independent of woman, nor woman independent of man, in the Lord. 12 For as woman [came] from man, even so man also [comes] through woman; but all things are from God. (1 Corinthians 11:11-12 NKJV, emphasis mine)

This "Nevertheless" is the Greek word, "plen." It is most often translated "but," and can also be translated, "except" or "but rather." It represents a contrast from what was stated before it. This is Paul's writing. He says, "In the Lord," contrasting what they were saying just previously, which was actually *not* in the Lord. Now look at verse 8 above, in The Section Under Examination. It states the exact opposite of what Paul said here in verses 11-12, that in the Lord man comes through woman (mothers), and that "all things are from God." Do you see why he said, "BUT" (or "Nevertheless") here? If not, it will become very clear.

I will simply state and then back up what The Section Under Examination actually is. It is Paul, quoting the Corinthians back to them and then opposing their statement. Now, if I am right—and I can prove that I am—this will free up multitudes of sincere Daughters of God regarding their physical hair. This will clear up misunderstanding. We have to treat this passage with extreme caution, like a scientist with the correct protective gloves to extract something valuable from a volatile environment. There is POWER in what we extract.

This passage can be a huge hole in the road if not handled with extreme care. Let's take a look at it again. This time imagine it as Paul stating back their words to them before answering:

4 Every man praying or prophesying, having [his] head covered, dishonors his head. 5 But every woman who prays or prophesies with [her] head uncovered dishonors her head, for that is one and the same as if her head were shaved. 6 For if a woman is not covered, let her also be shorn. But if it is shameful for a woman to be shorn or shaved, let her be covered. 7 For a man indeed ought not to cover [his] head, since he is the image and glory of God; but woman is the glory of man. 8 For man is not from woman, but woman from man. 9 Nor was man created for the woman, but woman for the

man. **10 For this reason the woman ought to have [a symbol of] authority on [her] head, because of the angels. (1 Corinthians 11:4-10 NKJV)**

Now let's look at Paul's response:

11 ["But" or "Nevertheless" or "But rather"], neither [is] man independent of woman, nor woman independent of man, in the Lord. 12 For as woman [came] from man, even so man also [comes] through woman; but all things are from God. (1 Corinthians 11:11-12 NKJV)

We saw earlier how this is a correction of verse 8 and 9 above. He goes on:

13 Judge among yourselves[:] Is it proper for a woman to pray to God with her head uncovered? 14 Does not even nature itself teach you that if a man has long hair, it is a dishonor to him? 15 But if a woman has long hair, it is a glory to her; for [her] hair is given to her for a covering. (1 Corinthians 11:13-15 NKJV)

Now this, right here also shows that he is opposing what they were saying. And again he contradicts verses found in the section above. He says that "her hair is given for a covering." But the verses above said that hair is not enough, that she should either "be covered" or shave her head. *The two ideas oppose each other.* Paul said her hair *IS* a covering, but the section above said she must be covered.

Next is the clincher. This proves what I have been saying completely:

16 But if anyone seems to be contentious, we have NO SUCH CUSTOM, nor [do] the churches of God. (1 Corinthians 11:16 NKJV, emphasis mine)

Notice the debate environment here. He's speaking to his students, answering their questions, clearing things up, and also shutting down those who want to argue. In the end he says, "We don't do that! Neither do any of the Churches of God around the world."

If you look back at the Section Under Examination, which we can now call, "The Debated Quotation," you'll see more issues with it. Apart from the general vibe and tone of it not matching Paul or the rest of Scripture, it also outright contradicts the Scripture. Verse 7 says that man is the image and glory of God but woman is the glory of man. Where is that in Scripture? Nowhere. On the other hand, Scripture says:

So God created man in His [own] image; in the image of God He created him; male and female He created them. (Genesis 1:27 NKJV)

[God] created them male and female, and He blessed them and named them Man in the day when they were created. (Genesis 5:2 NASB)

The "Man" that God created here, does not refer to sex but to the species, to the race of mankind. It includes "male and female." Both were still in the one "Man" when he was created *in the image of God*. Male and female were both created, together as one, in the image of God. Of course Paul knew that, and he wasn't deviating from Scripture. These were the words of the Corinthians, being quoted back to them.

Note that this verse 16 above, which is the absolute clincher of what I am saying, was *mistranslated* by several Bible versions. The KJV, NKJV, and ESV got it right: "no such custom." That is the clear Greek meaning and one possible meaning of the word "toioutos": "such as this, of this kind or sort." That is its *only* meaning. It's never, ever translated, "other"—the exact opposite meaning—except in this one passage, by the NIV, NLT, CSB, and NASB 1995[2] versions. This caused *confusion* as to the meaning of the entire passage! No doubt the enemy had a hand in this—he's deathly afraid of Women of God coming to their full glory, more than anything else. I'll share more as to why later.

Neither Paul, nor any other Legislature of God, had *such* a practice as they had described. He addressed and corrected it here.

---

[2] The NASB 2000 version corrected their earlier mistake, translating it accurately as "no such practice."

Chapter 2

Who Wrote Women Should Be Silent?

There are two other places that I know of in 1 Corinthians, where Paul quotes the Corinthians back to them, and answers what they had said. Here is one of them:

All things are lawful for me, but all things are not helpful. All things are lawful for me, but I will not be brought under the power of any. 13 Foods for the stomach and the stomach for foods, but God will destroy both it and them... (1 Corinthians 6:12-13 NKJV)

It seems clear to me that Paul was quoting the Corinthians when he said, "All things are lawful to me," and then he replied with a balancing statement. The same with "Foods for the stomach and the stomach for foods." These sound like they were likely popular sayings of the Corinthians, which Paul quoted and then commented on. I state this as another example of the unique dialogue Paul was having with the Corinthians in this unique letter.

Now let's deal with the other quotation he made of the Corinthians, revealing another flaw in their thinking regarding women. Understanding it will prepare God's People for growth and the supply of the clean water of the Word.

First let's start with Paul's words in 1 Corinthians 14 because we'll come back to these. We know that he is writing to men *and* women—to the whole Legislature ("Church") in Corinth—when he says:

Now I want [or "wish/desire"] you ALL to speak in tongues, but even more to prophesy. The one who prophesies is greater than the one who speaks in tongues, unless someone interprets, so that the church may be built up. (1 Corinthians 14:5 ESV, emphasis mine)
If, therefore, the whole church comes together and ALL speak in tongues, and outsiders or unbelievers enter, will they not say that you are out of your minds? 24 But if ALL prophesy, and an unbeliever or outsider enters, he is convicted by ALL, he is called to account by ALL, 25 the secrets of his heart are disclosed, and so, falling on his face, he will worship God and declare that God is really among you. (1 Corinthians 14:23-25 ESV, emphasis mine)

31 For you can ALL prophesy one by one, so that ALL may learn... 33 For God is not a God of confusion but of peace. As in all the churches of the saints, (1 Corinthians 14:31, 33 ESV, emphasis mine)

Now in the next verse all of the sudden he takes a detour. He makes a quick, seemingly strange statement, which was in fact a quote from them again. Then he refutes it swiftly and strongly:

34 the women should keep silent in the churches. For they are not permitted to speak, but should be in submission, as the Law also says.[3] 35 If there is anything they desire to learn, let them ask their husbands at home. For it is shameful for a woman to speak in church.

36 Or was it from you that the word of God came? Or are you the only ones it has reached? 37 If anyone thinks that he is a prophet, or spiritual, he should acknowledge that the things I am writing to you are a command of the Lord. 38 If anyone does not recognize this, he is not recognized. (1 Corinthians 14:34-38 ESV)

Do you see from verse 36 how he turns to refute verse 34-35? This is reminiscent of Chapter 11 when he said "we don't have any such practice, nor do the Legislatures of God!" Here he uses even stronger language!! He's addressing *their* arrogance. Obviously, he's not teaching them verse 34-35. But when people read only those two verses and assume Paul said it, they're making a big mistake.

What are "the things I am writing to you" in verse 37? They include the verses I quoted above that encouraged, "ALL" to speak, which includes men and women, just as on the Day of Pentecost when Jesus sent the Holy Spirit. He used some of his strongest

---

[3] Nowhere in the Law of Moses, nor any of the Books from Genesis to Malachi, is this idea stated, *ever*. Paul was an expert in the Law of Moses, and he wrote by the Holy Spirit. He would not make such a mistake as to say this. Verses 34-35 were the Corinthians' words.

words of all, in verse 38 (take another look)—this is very, very serious.

When we look at Bible verses, especially those that stand alone in the Bible, we must do so with caution and reverence for the Lord. We must examine the immediate context, the context of the book it's written in, and also the context of the whole Bible.

We have record of the doctrine and practice of the New Testament disciples. We should keep that whole in mind while considering individual passages. In Acts 2, Peter quoted Joel to explain the pouring out of the Holy Spirit they were receiving. He said,

But this is what was uttered through the prophet Joel: 17 "'And in the last days it shall be, God declares, that I will pour out my Spirit on all flesh, and your sons and your daughters shall prophesy, and your young men shall see visions, and your old men shall dream dreams; 18 even on my male servants and female servants in those days I will pour out my Spirit, and they shall prophesy. (Acts 2:16-18 ESV)

This is strong, clear language that sets the pace for the whole of the Book of Acts and the entire age we're living in, till Jesus returns. The Corinthians' idea contradicted and sought to prevent the fulfilment of this clear prophecy. So Paul opposed them.

What "custom" did "the Churches of God" have? It could not be clearer: "Even on my male servants and female servants…they shall prophesy." Paul also spoke this way in 1 Corinthians 14, in accord with the will of God revealed also through Joel and Peter.

Years later in Acts, we see an example of this lived

out:

On the next day we [I.e., Paul, Luke, etc.] departed and came to Caesarea, and we entered the house of Philip the evangelist, who was one of the seven, and stayed with him. 9 He had four unmarried daughters, who prophesied.[4] (Acts 21:8-9 ESV)

However, the Corinthians had their own idea, that women couldn't speak in the meetings, that doing so is "shameful." Then why would the Holy Spirit rest on them with tongues of fire, in Acts 2 and empower them to prophesy? And why did Paul say, to men and women, "You may all prophesy..."? Why are women prophetesses named if they are not allowed to speak, since the only way to prophesy is with speech? The Corinthians were severely mistaken. Paul had to ensure they all acknowledge that the things he was writing them—not the words quoted in verses 34-35, but of the whole chapter—were the command of the Lord. And these things were in accord with the rest of the New Testament.

The apostles were not sexist nor trying to silence half of the Body of Christ. They were encouragers of all to serve all, for the growth of all

For you can ALL prophesy one by one, so that all may learn and all be encouraged, (1 Corinthians 14:31 ESV)

As EACH ONE has received a gift, minister it to

---

[4] Or, "who were prophetesses," as the Greek suggests and the NASB translates it.

ONE ANOTHER, as good stewards of the manifold grace of God. 11 If ANYONE speaks, [let him speak] as the oracles of God. If ANYONE ministers, [let him do it] as with the ability which God supplies, that in all things God may be glorified through Jesus Christ, to whom belong the glory and the dominion forever and ever. Amen. (1 Peter 4:10-11 NKJV)

Now YOU are the body of Christ, and members individually. (1 Corinthians 12:27 NKJV)

...speaking the truth in love, we are to grow up in every way into him who is the head, into Christ, 16 from whom the WHOLE body, joined and held together by every joint with which it is equipped, when EACH PART is working properly, makes the body grow so that it builds itself up in love. (Ephesians 4:15-16 ESV)

The Lord gives the word; the women who announce the news are a great host [I.e., "army" or "multitude."][5] (Psalm 68:11 ESV)

---

[5] Women were the first evangelists, including in the first meeting after Jesus rose.

Author's Note:

This booklet is just a taste of a larger work, entitled, "Shine" ("Women, it is Your Time"), also by David O'Brien. "Shine" is currently available on Amazon and through our websites. If this booklet has blessed you, I encourage you to obtain and enjoy the full book also.

www.ThePurityForum.com

Life Changing Resources

Books by David O'Brien
- Shine – *ThePurityForum.com*
- Return to Acts Christianity – *ActsChristianity.com*
- Heal The Sick – *ActsChristianity.com*
- For Freedom – *ThePurityForum.com*

By Sonia O'Brien
- Kingdom Rich
- Twenty-Five Words

FOR FREEDOM RADIO – *ForFreedomRadio.com*
- Podcast/Radio Show Hosted by David O'Brien
- Including my songs, "For Freedom," "Made to Fly," & "Loyalty"

ThePurityForum.com – *Coming Soon!*
- A treasure chest of resources on freedom, relationships, marriage, sexuality, and family
- Home also to *The Purity Alliance* network

EMPOWER MEDIA NETWORK
- This is our TV network, "Empowering you to empower others."
- Available on Roku TV, Apple TV, Fire TV and at www.EmpowerMediaNetwork.com

www.BlueDiamondBookhouse.com

Kingdom Rich

Sonia O'Brien

FOR FREEDOM

How God Freed You from Slavery

Iesus Nazarenus rex Iudaeorum

DAVID O'BRIEN

FORFREEDOMRADIO.COM

IT WAS
FOR
FREEDOM...

LIBERATING...

LIFE-GIVING...

DIVINELY
POWERFUL!

HEAL THE SICK

Gospel Healing
Teaching for The New Man

DAVID O'BRIEN

RETURN TO
ACTS CHRISTIANITY

The Reformation God & His People
are Yearning for - *Beyond the Walls
of Traditional Church Structure*

David O'Brien

www.ingramcontent.com/pod-product-compliance
Lightning Source LLC
Chambersburg PA
CBHW060707280326
41933CB00012B/2337